Ancient Roman Children

Richard Tames

H **www.heinemann.co.uk/library**
Visit our website to find out more information about **Heinemann Library** books.

To order:
☎ Phone 44 (0) 1865 888066
▤ Send a fax to 44 (0) 1865 314091
▭ Visit the Heinemann Bookshop at www.heinemann.co.uk/library to browse our catalogue and order online.

First published in Great Britain by Heinemann Library, Halley Court, Jordan Hill, Oxford OX2 8EJ, part of Harcourt Education. Heinemann is a registered trademark of Harcourt Education Ltd.

Designed by Tinstar Design (www.tinstar.co.uk)
Illustrated by Jeff Edwards
Originated by Ambassador Litho Ltd
Printed in China by Wing King Tong

ISBN 0 431 14552 0 (hardback)
06 05 04 03 02
10 9 8 7 6 5 4 3 2 1

ISBN 0 431 14555 5 (paperback)
07 06 05 04 03
10 9 8 7 6 5 4 3 2 1

British Library Cataloguing in Publication Data
Tames, Richard
    Ancient Roman children. – (People in the past)
    1. Children – Rome – History – Juvenile literature
    2. Civilization, Modern – Roman influences – Juvenile literature
    3. Rome – Social conditions – 510–30 B.C. – Juvenile literature
    I.Title
    305.2'3'0937

Acknowledgements
The Publisher would like to thank the following for permission to reproduce photographs:
AKG Photos pp18, 23, 28; Ancient Art & Architecture Collection pp6, 7, 16, 20, 22, 26, 27, 30, 41; Art Directors & TRIP/Carlos Chinca p14; C M Dixon pp8, 39; Colchester Museums p15; English Heritage Photo Library/Corbridge Museum p25; Sonia Halliday p32; Michael Holford p40; Museum of London Archaeological Service pp42, 43; Scala Art Resource pp9, 10, 12, 24; John Seely pp17, 34; Trevor Clifford p29; Werner Foreman Archive pp36, 38.

Cover photograph reproduced with permission of Corbis.

Every effort has been made to contact copyright holders of any material reproduced in this book. Any omissions will be rectified in subsequent printings if notice is given to the Publisher.

Contents

Words appearing in the text in bold, **like this**, are explained in the Glossary.

The Roman world

From city to empire

Ancient Rome began as a city and grew into an **empire**, stretching from Italy as far as Scotland, Spain, Sudan and Syria. As Rome expanded, so did Roman law and Rome's language, Latin.

As the capital of the empire, Rome was the hub of its excellent road system. It grew to become a city of a million people, by far the largest in the world the Romans knew. Respect for the **emperor**, obedience to Roman law, and superbly trained Roman armies held the huge empire together. For centuries the vast army protected the empire against **barbarian** raiders on its borders.

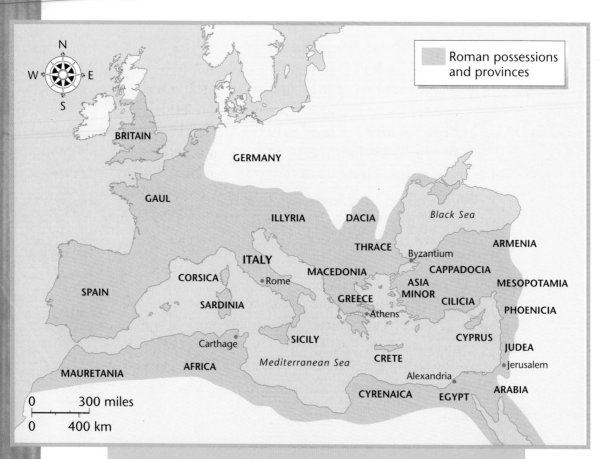

This map shows the Roman world in AD 100, when the empire was at its biggest. In many lands, families under Roman rule copied Roman ways, and lived in Roman-style homes.

Latin, languages and learning

Roman civilization lasted over a thousand years. Latin, the Roman language, later developed into other languages including Italian, French, Spanish, Portuguese and Romanian. Even English, a **Germanic** language, owes a third of its words to Latin. Some, like 'exit' (he goes), or 'veto' (I forbid) are still completely Latin in form. Latin remained the language of learning throughout Europe until about 1800. It still remains the official language of the Roman Catholic Church to this day. Species (another Latin word!) of plants, birds and animals are still recognized around the world by their Latin names.

Rome all around

Modern roads still follow routes first surveyed and built by Roman engineers. In Britain they built 6000 miles of roads within 40 years of their conquest. Many sections of Roman city walls still stand. London, Paris, Milan, Lyons and Cologne were all founded by Romans. Most European countries' legal systems are still based on Roman law. Roman history has inspired plays by Shakespeare, operas by Verdi and films by Hollywood. We can also thank the Romans for banks, fire brigades and public hospitals. They also gave us blocks of flats and proper drains, as well as central heating, glass windows, concrete and our calendar.

Rome's children

The Romans liked to have large families, with many children. But Roman couples were often saddened by the death of their children before they were old enough to marry and have children of their own. We know far less about the lives of Roman children than we do about their parents. This book is about explaining why this is, and what we do know.

Invisible children of Rome

◀▷ ◀▷ ◀▷ ◀▷ ◀▷ ◀▷ ◀▷ ◀▷ ◀▷ ◀▷ ◀▷ ◀▷ ◀▷ ◀▷ ◀▷ ◀▷

One way to find out about Roman children is by reading what people wrote about them. Some important Roman writers, like Horace, Cicero and Pliny, did write about children, but obviously they wrote from an adult's point of view. Usually they wrote about how children ought to behave, rather than how they actually did behave. Women spent more time with children than men did, but women rarely wrote. Roman laws set out the rights and duties of children in detail. The laws, however, are more evidence of how life ought to have been, rather than how it really was.

Time warp

In AD 79 a volcanic eruption of Mount Vesuvius destroyed the seaside towns of Pompeii and Herculaneum. Buildings as well as bodies were buried beneath a layer of lava over 4 metres deep. Pliny the Younger, an eyewitness, described the event in two letters to the historian Tacitus. **Excavations** that began in the 1700s have uncovered half of Pompeii, including documents preserved in a chest, and paintings on walls. These finds tell us about the lives of Roman families and children.

The homes of rich Romans were decorated with wall paintings, like this one, often showing scenes from everyday life – but not the everyday life of the poor.

A statue of Romulus and Remus as babies, with the she-wolf who brought them up.

Recovering the past

Pompeii was a resort town where many wealthy Romans had homes for holidays, or their retirement. This means that what has been found there may not be typical of the way of life of the average Roman. Excavations of poor people's homes in the port of Ostia, near Rome, probably provide better evidence of this.

Romulus and Remus

Roman **myths**, like the one about Romulus and Remus, the legendary founders of Rome also convey ideas about childhood. They were left to die at birth, but brought up by a wolf. When they grew up they began building a city where the wolf had found them. The brothers quarrelled, and Romulus killed Remus and called the city after himself. This story tells us that Romans clearly admired children who were survivors. Romulus was said to have made a law that Romans should raise all their boys and the first-born girl.

The building of an extension to London's underground system meant cutting through a Roman layer of **archaeology**. It uncovered a road rutted by the wheels of Roman carts, traces of a wood-lined tank for keeping oysters, a storage jar for fish sauce from Spain and a pottery lamp shaped like a foot. Previous Roman remains found in London have included a teenage girl's leather bikini.

Being born

By law Roman girls could marry at the age of twelve. The usual age was around fourteen. Girls were supposed to have children as soon as they married, and go on having more. It was believed that the younger the mother, the safer the birth. In fact very young girls were as much at risk as older women, weakened by many births. More Roman women died in childbirth than Roman men were killed in war.

To live or to die?
Roman fathers wanted boys rather than girls. It was essential to have a boy to inherit family property, carry on the family name and care for the family's tombs. Girls could not add to the family income by working, and when they married they had to be given a **dowry**. When a baby was born it was bathed and then placed at the father's feet for his approval. If he picked it up, the child was accepted into the family.

Boy or girl, a baby had to be healthy and without defects or deformities. Sickly or disabled babies could legally be left out to die of cold and hunger. It was strictly illegal to bring abandoned babies up as **slaves** if they had been born free. However, **slave**

This carving on a stone coffin in Rome shows a mother and a slave woman bathing a baby. It is possible that this coffin belongs to either a mother or a baby.

The *bulla*

A good luck charm called a *bulla* was hung around the neck of a newborn baby as a protection against illness, accident and witchcraft. Romans believed that witches kidnapped and killed babies to use their body parts in making spells. In rich families the *bulla* was made of gold, in poor families it was leather. This would be worn until the child became an adult.

traders often picked them up. Girls were more likely to be rejected, especially if a family already had one. Sometimes children were sold to slave traders, or given to families needing to adopt an **heir**, simply because parents were too poor to bring them up.

Dangerous years

The happy news of the birth of a healthy child was often painted on the outside wall of the family home. The whole neighbourhood could then offer congratulations and prayers for good fortune. It is probable that of every ten children born alive, three would die before reaching their first birthday. Another three would die before passing ten. This was because disease was common in busy Roman cities, and doctors knew less about treating and curing disease than they do today. A couple would usually need to have at least five children if two were to survive to have children of their own.

These three *bullas* from the 4th century AD would have been worn by children born to rich parents.

Bringing up baby

Infant care

Our word 'infant' comes from the Latin *'in fans'* meaning 'without speech'. Romans believed babies were like modelling clay that needed moulding to the correct shape. So they were **swaddled** tightly with cloths, especially around the joints. Their limbs were often put in splints to make them grow straight. The right hand was freed from binding first to make sure that the child grew up right-handed. Left-handedness was thought to be unlucky. Our word 'sinister' is from the Latin for 'left'. Babies were also given daily cold baths to toughen them.

This fine tombstone was put up by a sad husband in memory of his wife, who died in childbirth. The **inscription** in Latin introduces her to the ghosts of the **Underworld**.

DIS MANIBVS TI CLAVDI DIONYSI
FECIT CLAVDIA PREPONTIS PATRONO
BENEMERENTI SIBI ET SVIS
POSTERISQVE EORVM

The high rate of infant death encouraged Roman mothers to make offerings to a whole range of **protective gods** and goddesses. These included Vaticanus who opened a baby's mouth for its first scream, Vitumnus who controlled breathing, Sentinus the senses, Ruminus breast-feeding, Potina drinking and Educa eating. Cumina watched over cradles, and Parentia drove away things like bad dreams. Carna warded off stomach infections – **dysentery** from dirty water was almost certainly a major killer of babies. Romans blamed dysentery on evil spirits called *Strigae*. To keep them out, babies' bedrooms had narrow, slit windows guarded by sprigs of prickly hawthorn that the spirits would find hard to get past.

The *paedogogue*

Children in slave-owning households often had a male childminder called a *paedogogue*. He would play with them, take them to the **public baths** and generally keep them out of trouble. He would teach them table manners and, if he could read, the alphabet. In any case he would escort the children to school and stay there, reporting back to their parents on their behaviour. Romans believed in strict discipline. Even small children could expect to be punished for tantrums, sulking or disobedience.

Nurses and nannies

Rich Roman women often refused to breast-feed their babies themselves. Instead they hired **wet nurses** to do this for them. Soranus, a Greek doctor working in Rome, advised hiring a nurse of at least twenty, with two or three children of her own. This should ensure she was experienced and sensible. He also suggested Greek nurses, because it was thought that the baby would then grow up speaking Greek as well as Latin! A successful wet nurse might be kept on to become a nanny. **Divorce** was common among wealthy Romans, and children stayed with their father. This meant that many Roman children grew up closer to their nanny than to their mother.

Family life

Our word 'family' comes from the Latin *familia*, meaning household. A Roman household would include a married couple, their children and often other relatives, such as older, childless aunts, uncles or cousins. A wealthy household would also have included **slaves** owned by the head of the family.

One big, happy family

Romans liked large families. Family members could help each other in work and **politics**, so the bigger a family, the richer and more powerful it could become. The more children one had, the better chance there was some would survive to look after their parents when they were old. Wealth was no guarantee of health. Cornelia, mother of the **emperor** Tiberius, had twelve babies but only three survived to grow up.

This Roman couple look quite old to have the young boy shown between them.

When a grown child died as a teenager, poor parents felt that they had been cheated out of security in their old age. They also thought they had lost the time and money they had spent on bringing the child up for years. If a married couple failed to have children of their own, or lost them through illness or accident, they often adopted one or more.

Father knows best

In early Roman times fathers had complete power over their families. They even had the right to kill their children if they were disobedient! Wherever possible, different generations lived together in the same house. The oldest living male was the head of the family. This meant that, if a middle-aged man's father was still alive, he still had to get his permission for important decisions like getting married or selling a house or farm.

Mother dearest

The duty of the mother was to have children, bring them up and organize the household. Respectable women did not leave the house much. They might go out to visit a female friend in her home, or take part in a religious occasion for females. **Slaves** went out for the everyday shopping at the market and shops. Wives were expected to have as many children as possible. Every time a woman had a child she risked death. There were no clean hospitals to give birth in, and doctors and **midwives** lacked much of the knowledge that modern doctors have. Many wives died in their twenties or thirties, and so husbands might remarry two or three times. **Divorce** was allowed under Roman law, but when a couple separated the children stayed with their father. This meant many children were brought up by stepmothers and, among the rich, by nurses or nannies.

House and home

The rich

Wealthy town children were kept mostly at home for fear of disease, accident or other harm. They lived in single-storey detached houses with thick, high walls, small, shuttered windows and a guarded doorway for security. Rooms ran round an open, airy courtyard (*atrium*) with a pool for rainwater. This would be a safe and shady place to play with toys, dolls or pets such as dogs and cats. The dining room, used for entertaining, was usually the grandest room in the house. There was often a study or library for the master of the house. Children were usually kept out of these rooms except on special occasions like family celebrations. Big houses had a rear courtyard (*peristyle*) with a garden, sometimes used as an outdoor dining room. The best houses had piped water and underfloor central heating. Tile or **mosaic** floors were good for games like marbles.

Wealthy families usually had a country **villa** for summer. Here they could entertain friends, and get away from the heat and noise of the city. Children would have more freedom to play in the farmyard, go fishing or hunt birds and small animals.

This villa in Pompeii would have belonged to a very wealthy family. Children would have plenty of room to play in the gardens here.

These items were found in a child's grave. Many Roman children died because of disease.

The poor

Most ordinary townsfolk lived in apartment blocks. They were usually three or four floors in height, and known as *insulae* (islands). The ground floor, usually made of stone or brick, had shops, restaurants and public toilets for residents. The higher floors were often very flimsy. The poor families lived here, often in a single room. Space for children to play was very limited. *Insulae* had no water supply, drainage or heating. They were packed close together, and the air was poor. Sickness spread easily. Water came from public fountains, and waste was thrown out of the window into the street. Because of this, children risked catching illnesses in the dirty streets. Residents suffered from smoke, smells, noise and danger from fire.

Meals

Most Romans lived in warm climates, and most food was eaten cold. Bread, fish, eggs, chicken, olives, fruit, nuts and beans were staple foods. Only children and sick people drank milk, as most of it was used to make cheese. Older children drank wine or vinegar watered down. Butter was used to soothe babies with teething pains or mouth ulcers. At the main evening meal, wealthy adults ate while lying on couches. Children and the poor sat on stools. Even the rich ate with their fingers. Poor people ate from food shops selling porridge, pies, fritters, soups and sausages. This was because they had no kitchens at home.

Learning for life

In the days of the Roman **republic** fathers were supposed to take the time to educate their sons themselves, teaching them everything from writing to riding. Girls learned the domestic skills they needed to know at home, from their mother and the household **slaves**.

After the Romans conquered Greece, they took over many Greek ways. They began to send their sons out to elementary school at the age of six or seven, until they were eleven or twelve. Girls might go too, but not past the age of twelve. Boys from wealthy families who expected them to go into **politics** went on studying for as many as ten more years. If they failed to make the grade, and were thought unfit to represent the family in the law courts or as a government official, they might be sent to live at a country **villa**. Here they would pass their lives overseeing the farm work.

The uses of literacy

It was thought that every free Roman male ought to be able to keep household accounts, read a **legal contract**, and keep written records of family prayers, remedies and farming tips.

A Roman gravestone from the 1st–2nd century AD, in Ostia, Italy. It begins with the greeting *Dis Manibus*, which means 'To the Ghosts of the Dead' and then introduces the person buried there.

The Forum at Pompeii today. Whole streets of Pompeii and Herculaneum have been uncovered by centuries of patient **excavation**.

Girls from wealthy families might also find reading and writing very helpful because that would show that their family was respectable. This meant it was very useful to keep in touch with their friends and relatives by means of letters. They also had the time to teach their daughters this useful skill. Because Latin was written without punctuation, it was necessary to read it aloud to make sure the reader understood where each sentence began and ended. Being able to read aloud meant being able to entertain, or help other members of the family.

Domestic skills

Girls had to learn how to cook, and how to **spin** yarn and **weave** it into cloth. Girls in poorer families would actually need these skills when they got married. Girls of rich families would have a chef to cook for them, and could buy clothes for their family, rather than make them. They still had to know how these things were done. They could then check up that their slaves were not cheating them, or skimping on their work. Even the daughters of the **emperor** himself were taught how to spin and weave.

Schools and teachers

Primary

Elementary schools focused on basic reading, writing and arithmetic. The teacher was often an ex-**slave**, or disabled ex-soldier. Elementary school teachers were poorly paid, and not much respected by the general public. One Roman writer complained that by shouting at pupils arriving late the teacher often woke up people nearby who were still trying to sleep! The teacher's payment depended on the number of pupils he could attract and keep. Classes were usually small, only up to around twelve. Apart from fees, teachers also expected gifts at major **festivals**.

Romans expected that children would not like learning, and would therefore need beating regularly. Paintings show a pupil was often lifted onto the back of one of his classmates to be beaten with a cane, or eel-skin strap. Modern ideas about learning for fun, or through encouragement, would have seemed strange to Roman thinking.

Roman books, like the one held by the young man in the picture, were written on scrolls of parchment made from animal skins. Books were too expensive for children to have their own copies, so they would have to learn text by heart.

What did writers say about school?

The Roman writer Quintilian said that children – particularly only children – should be sent to school because if they stayed at home they would grow up spoiled and rude. Another writer, Seneca, agreed – 'A child will not stand up to hardships in life if he has not been denied anything and has always had his tears wiped away by his mother.'

There were no school buildings as such. Lessons were given in the open air, or in a hired room, often at the back of a shop. The teacher sat in a chair, the pupils on benches. The day lasted from dawn until early afternoon, with a break for lunch. Pupils had religious festivals off, plus every ninth day.

Learning at home

Boys from wealthy families active in **politics** had to learn both Latin and Greek. Many were taught by tutors at home. This did not necessarily mean learning alone. They were often part of a class consisting of brothers, cousins, the sons of neighbours and even favoured slaves who might go on to become secretaries, librarians or family tutors themselves. Teachers at this level, dealing with boys aged from twelve until their late teens, were much better paid and treated with general respect.

Higher education

The third stage of education was public speaking, known as **rhetoric**. Very rich families might even send their sons to Athens or Crete to study under famous Greek teachers. The great Roman lawyer Cicero was a student until he was thirty. Public speaking was essential for those who wanted to enter public life as lawyers or politicians.

Lessons and learning

Writing and reciting

The Roman alphabet was based on the Greek one, although the actual letters looked more like the ones used to write English today. The first thing children were taught was the Greek alphabet. This was because it was harder than Latin, and so they would then find learning the Latin alphabet easy. First they were taught the names of the letters. Then how to recite them forwards. Then how to recite them backwards – and only then what they actually looked like!

At the bottom of this Roman coin are the letters SPQR which stand for Senate (Government) and People of Rome. The Latin is *Senatus Populusque Romanus*.

Writing equipment

Pupils learned writing on wooden boards that were covered with a thin layer of wax. Letters were scratched on with a pointed **stylus**. The flat end of the stylus was used for crossing out mistakes, and smoothing over the wax for re-use. More advanced students would learn to write on papyrus, a kind of paper imported from Egypt. They used a reed pen, and ink made from soot and gum. Papyrus could be scrubbed clean and used several times.

Pupils were also expected to learn long sections of verse by heart, and recite them aloud. These were often stories about the gods or heroes from Roman history. They also learned rhymes about useful things, such as the value of different kinds of coin.

For children aged eleven and above, the curriculum concentrated on poetry and essay writing. There was also some geography, history, music and **astronomy**. A lot of teaching consisted of the teacher posing a series of questions, and the pupil responding with correct answers that they had to memorise.

Public speaking

A confident use of language was essential for those commanding soldiers, presenting cases in the law courts and running for election to public office. Cicero, who became one of the greatest Roman public speakers, taught himself to overcome a stammer by practising speaking with a stone in his mouth. This made him control his breathing and say each word clearly.

Students of **rhetoric** had to learn how to put forward an argument, train their memory and use gestures and tricks of speech effectively. They memorised famous speeches and debated legal cases. One of the first public occasions on which a young man might try out his speaking skills would be making a speech in praise of a dead relative at their funeral.

Figure it out

Children needed to know arithmetic to buy things in the market. Children of farmers, merchants, shopkeepers and craftsmen also needed to learn how to measure and weigh things as well. Children of rich families might also learn geometry because the Greeks did it, so it was fashionable. Boys aiming to follow their father as an architect, engineer, surveyor or boat-builder also needed to learn geometry.

Mathematics

Romans used seven symbols to write numbers – I (=1) V (=5) X (=10) L (=50) C (=100) D (=500) and M (=1000). They could be used to write any other number, and were easier to carve in stone or wood than the numbers we use today. Roman numerals were written with the highest value on the left, and smallest on the right. Therefore MDCCCCLVIII = 1000 + 500 + (4 x 100) + 50 + 5 + (3 x 1) = 1958. When a smaller number symbol occurs to the left of a larger one it is subtracted: 9 is written IX, and 4 as IV. Numbers over one thousand were written by putting a line above a numeral. Multiplication and division were so difficult with Roman numerals they were left to clerks. Merchants used a counting-board called an abacus, with vertical columns and counters to represent numbers.

A Roman merchant's abacus, which clearly shows the counters that represented numbers.

Weights and measures

The standard Roman unit of weight was the *libra* or pound. It was equivalent to 327.45 grams. The *libra* was divided into twelve ounces. The Roman foot, divided into twelve inches, was equal to 11.65 modern inches (29.6 cm). Five feet were called one pace, and a thousand paces were one mile. The Roman mile equalled 1618.5 yards (1480 metres) and was therefore shorter than the modern mile of 1760 yards. Roman military roads were lined with milestones to help army commanders pace their soldiers' marching. It would have been important for children to understand weights and measures when they started work, or served across the **empire** in the Roman army.

A hoard of Roman coins dating from the 1st–3rd century AD.

Money

Another use for the maths that Roman children learned would be in counting money. The smallest coin was an *as*. Four *asses* made one *sestertius*, and four *sesterces* made one *denarius*. A small sack of wheat cost eight *sesterces*. A character in a novel by the writer Petronius described the importance of learning these things: 'I didn't learn geometry and literary criticism and useless nonsense like that … I learned how to divide things into hundreds and work out percentages, and I know weights, measures and currency.'

Toys

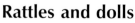

Rattles and dolls

Parents or other family members probably made most of their toys. Children in rich families might have toys made by skilled craftsmen. Babies were given clappers or rattles made of wood, clay pottery or bone. Some had loose pebbles inside. Toddlers had wooden trolleys on wheels to push along, to help them learn to walk.

Dolls were made out of cloth and wax. They often had movable arms and legs. Models and farmyard and pet animals were made out of clay, wood or bronze. Metal hoops and wooden wheels were used for bowling along. Some had bells on, so that they made a jingling noise. This also warned people to get out of the way!

Older children's toys

There were also wooden **hobby horses**, and toy **chariots** with sails on to make them go faster. A rich child might have a chariot big enough to be pulled along by a goat, or a pair of geese. At the other end of the scale were carts drawn by mice, that were raced against each other. Marbles were made of pottery or glass. Country children often used hazelnuts or walnuts instead. Older children had whips and tops, kites, swings, see-saws and go-karts. Boys fenced with wooden swords.

A Roman doll. The doll has movable joints, which is a similar idea to dolls that are played with now. It is likely that this would have belonged to a child from a wealthy family.

Making a ball

Although rubber and plastics were unknown to the Romans, there were a number of ways of making a ball that could bounce. One was to blow up a pig's bladder, and wrap it tightly inside a protective outer cover of animal skin or leather. Another was to use catgut, or some other kind of animal **sinew** wound together like a ball of string, also covered with skin or leather. A third method was to use bits of natural sponge held together by string, and then wrapped in cloth. Sponge balls would not bounce nearly as well as the other kinds, but were much easier to make.

Roman children, and also grown-ups, played many different kinds of ball game, so balls of different kinds were very common. Some were hard, and used for bowling or catching. There were even balls made of glass. These, of course, could break and so were used in catching games that needed a high level of skill. Young children would probably not have been allowed to use them. Younger children played with soft balls made of rags, or hair wrapped inside **linen**.

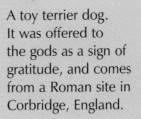

A toy terrier dog. It was offered to the gods as a sign of gratitude, and comes from a Roman site in Corbridge, England.

Games

Ball games

Many Roman ball games are known about, but the exact rules are not. One children's game involved two **concentric circles** drawn on the ground. The inner one was 1.5 metres across, and the outer one 6 metres across. Three or more players stood outside the outer ring and threw the ball to each other by bouncing it into the inner circle. If the ball was not caught one-handed the thrower got a point. Whoever caught the ball threw it next. Players could run round the outer circle. The first player to score 21 points won the game.

The game *Trigon* involved three catchers standing in a triangle, 6 metres apart. It must have been fast because a separate scorer was needed. Sometimes two hard balls were in play at the same time. There may have been a rule about throwing with one hand, and having to catch with the other. Points might also have been won for catching a ball, and extra points won for palming it on. Points were lost for dropping the ball, and the winning score was again 21.

A carving relief of children playing, from the 2nd century AD. Evidence of many different kinds of game survives, but it is often difficult to work out what the rules were.

Gambling, throwing and guessing

Children and adults played with dice. **Gambling** was illegal, except during the **festival** of Saturnalia. Knucklebones was a favourite game with girls. These were long and narrow animal bones, with two flat faces, one concave face and one convex face. The ends did not count. The four faces were valued one, three, four and six. Using four knucklebones there were thirty-five scoring combinations a player could throw. The top score was when each bone thrown showed a different number – 1, 3, 4 and 6.

Nuts were often used for throwing games. One involved trying to throw nuts into a narrow-necked container. Another required players to throw a nut onto a carefully arranged pile of nuts without making the pile collapse.

Another game, still played in southern Italy until recent times, involved two players each raising their right hand at the same time and guessing the total number of fingers raised by both players. There were also several different kinds of board game. They either involved capturing pieces like modern chess or draughts, or racing counters to an end-point, like backgammon.

A mosaic of men playing dice, possibly gambling. Children would also play dice, but would certainly not have taken part in any gambling.

Sports

Taking part

The Romans had immense respect for Greek learning, but they did not make competitive sport a major part of education, as the Greeks did. Boys, however, were expected to take part in sports as pastimes. These included such Greek favourites as wrestling, boxing and throwing the javelin. They also played very rough games. One involved two boys holding either end of a long rope, who then ran after two others, aiming to tie them up. The other two had sticks to beat off their pursuers. In the countryside hunting was used to build up toughness, test bravery against wild animals and gain skill with a spear. Riding was done without **stirrups**, which were still unknown.

Perhaps the boy at the bottom of the picture (right) sneaked in to watch the chariot racing?

Spectators

As the **empire** grew richer, the Romans began to leave serious sport to professionals. Fights between **gladiators** began as a form of human **sacrifice** at the funeral of an important person. Under the empire, gladiatorial games were big business. They were usually held at religious **festivals**. Many gladiators were criminals or **prisoners of war**, the rest were **slaves**. A tough teenage boy slave might be picked out by his owner to train as a future gladiator. Although becoming a gladiator was very dangerous, it did offer a slim hope of fame, freedom and fortune.

Boy racers

Chariot racing was as popular as watching gladiators, and almost as dangerous. Races between four different teams – the Reds, Blues, Whites and Greens – might involve up to twelve chariots. Smashes were frequent and often fatal. Whichever chariot finished first won – even without its driver! Top charioteers were sporting super-heroes. Many of the drivers were just boys when they began. Some started as young as twelve. Young charioteers were valued because the lighter the charioteer, the faster the chariot could travel. In a ten-year career ending with his death at the age of 22, African-born charioteer Crescens took part in 680 races. He won 47 victories, and prize money of 1,558,346 *sesterces*.

The Colosseum in Rome could hold 50,000 spectators. Boys were taken to gladiator fights here to toughen them up.

The world of work

Helping at home
Regular jobs for children included looking after younger brothers and sisters, keeping the fire going, fetching water and grinding grain to make flour. In the countryside they also gathered firewood, nuts, berries and mushrooms, cleared stones from fields and helped to harvest grapes and olives.

Following mum and dad
Most boys were brought up to do the same job as their father did, learning the trade from him. There were few jobs outside the home for women – **midwife**, shopkeeper, bath attendant, needlewoman or shepherdess. Most girls learned housekeeping skills from their mother. **Inscriptions** found on tombs show that some girls worked from a very young age: 'In memory of Pieris a hairdresser. She lived nine years. Her mother Hilara put up this tombstone.'

A banqueting scene from Pompeii. The children here are slaves and are attending to the adults.

Free citizens

In Rome itself there was a large class of free Roman **citizens**, around 150,000. They had no work, but were entitled by law to free food provided by the government. There was also a special extra feeding programme for the children of poor Romans, providing they were full citizens. This was begun so that poor families' sons could grow up to become soldiers.

Slavery

Slavery was common throughout the Roman world. A child born to a **slave** mother was by law a slave even if the father was free. Some slaves were captured **prisoners of war**. Others, often children, were bought from **slave traders** who had kidnapped them.

Household slaves

Most Roman households would have included slaves. These may well have included children who would have helped with cleaning and worked in the kitchen. In some houses, they would have been taught to read and write so they could be used for skilled jobs in later life. Many slaves were treated as valued members of the family and given positions of trust such as **physician**, teacher, bookkeeper or bodyguard. Others were musicians, hairdressers and cooks.

Industrial slaves

Slaves were often used for dirty, dangerous or exhausting work such as farming, making bricks, building and mining. Slave children were especially useful in mining for crawling through narrow tunnels. Mine slaves were treated brutally, and had many accidents. Runaway slaves who were caught could be branded or executed. Slaves were often forced to wear an iron collar to show that they were slaves.

Clothes and fashions

Roman clothing changed very little over a thousand years. Most children wore simple clothes of wool and **linen**, made at home by their mothers or **slaves**. The rich bought cloth ready-made, and could afford dyed materials and cottons from India. Cotton and silk were much lighter and more comfortable in warm climates, and could be washed and dried more easily. Women wore lighter, brighter colours and more patterns than men did. Children dressed even more simply than adults did, in loose **tunics**, sandals and cloaks. Girls usually only wore white until they were married. In cold climates, like Roman Britain, furs and felt were worn.

This mosaic, from Carthage, shows a young boy dressed in a short tunic.

The toga

When a boy wore a **toga** for the first time it meant he was grown-up. The toga was a large half-circle of thick white wool which had to be draped and folded with great care. Only adult male Roman **citizens** were allowed to wear a toga. A slave usually helped his master put it on, but it was awkward and heavy to wear. Most men preferred a tunic for everyday use. Successive **emperors** passed laws ordering men to wear a toga on formal occasions.

Garments

Because needles made of bronze or bone were rather clumsy, Roman clothes usually required little sewing. Boys and girls both wore **loincloths** as underwear, and a short tunic gathered at the waist. In warm weather tunics served as pyjamas as well. In colder weather they were used as underwear, and another heavier tunic was worn on top. In winter and wet weather cloaks, often hooded, were worn.

There were no buttons, and garments were held together with belts, drawstrings or pins. Children might carry knucklebones in the folds of their clothes. Coins were small and often carried in the mouth because garments had no pockets.

Fashion

Women wore robes reaching down to their ankles. They often covered their head with a veil, scarf or shawl outdoors to protect their hairstyle. Some wore wigs. These were made from black human hair brought over from India, or cut off from one of their own blonde slaves. Rich ladies with time on their hands spent hours on their appearance. Girls would learn from their mother or her maid how to choose jewellery, arrange their hair and put on make-up and perfume.

Keeping clean and healthy

Hygiene at home

In Roman **mythology** Hygieia, goddess of health, was the daughter of Aesculapius, god of healing. Her name gives us the word 'hygiene'. Although larger houses had pools and fountains for washing, most children would not have had a bathroom in their own homes. Toilets would often have been shared between families, particularly in poorer areas. People would have visited the **public baths**, where they could keep clean, meet friends and play ball or board games.

The public baths

Wherever possible the Romans built public bathhouses. They were used by the whole family. Children were allowed in free. The grandest baths had lead-lined pools, marble walls, **mosaic** floors and were decorated with statues and fountains. They were leisure, fitness and social centres with their own exercise yard, gymnasium, covered walks, gardens and shops. Children could keep fit at the same time as they kept clean. Cakes, biscuits, sausages and drinks were sold from street stalls.

The *palaestrum* (gym) at Pompeii, where young men prepared for athletic events, and used the large swimming pool on the right.

A concerned mother

This was written in Roman Egypt by a woman whose grown-up son was working away from home. It shows that mothers worried about their children, even when they had grown up: '[Your boss] told me you had hurt your foot on a piece of sharp wood. I was very worried you could only walk about slowly and with difficulty … if you know that you are not well, write to me and I will come … Your children send love …'.

Even children of rich families, with baths at home, went to the public baths. Most people went daily, women usually in the morning, and men in the afternoon after work. Children would probably have gone during the day, unless they were working. Daily bathing probably helped prevent skin diseases and heal minor cuts.

Before washing themselves in the baths, children would do some exercise in the gymnasium attached to the baths. They might practise wrestling, or throwing a ball to one another. The Romans believed, as we do, that exercise was an important part of staying healthy.

Health and death

Children, especially in dirty, overcrowded slums, could die from infectious diseases that were especially common in hot weather. In poor country areas, bad harvests caused deaths from underfeeding. Other fatal dangers included snakebites and accidents causing major wounds or broken bones which penetrated the skin. Most families were too poor to afford a doctor or lived too far away from one. Children relied on their parents to treat them with medicines made from herbs, oil, vinegar and honey.

Beliefs and behaviour

Inside the family home

The whole family would have been expected to worship the household gods every day. Each household had it's own **shrine** for family worship, led by the father. The shrine was called the *lararium*. Boys would learn what to do by copying their father, and when they had grown up they would have to lead their own family's worship. Girls might join their mother in making an offering to Vesta, goddess of the **hearth**, who was especially important to housewives.

A shrine to the household gods in Pompeii. In the centre stands the Genius, wearing a veil for offering a sacrifice.

Morals

The Romans brought their children up to follow duty, discipline and dignity in the face of life's trials. A Greek schoolmaster who taught Roman children made his pupils practise writing by copying out sayings like: 'Look to a wise man for advice,' and 'Do not blindly trust your friends'. He hoped that they would remember these phrases in later life.

Respect was shown to the gods by **sacrificing** animals or birds. They would also make offerings of **incense**, bread, fruit or wine and say prayers. Families were also watched over by a guardian spirit, and the spirits of their **ancestors**. Portraits or wax **death masks** of ancestors were placed around the *atrium*. Children's first experiences of religion would come from these ceremonies inside the home.

Children and the gods

The gods of the official religion were honoured at temples, and by public ceremonies in which children also took part. These usually involved a procession, then a sacrifice and prayers. Children learned the **myths** about the gods' adventures and quarrels. Many of the Roman gods they learned about were the same as those of ancient Greece but they had different names. Zeus, the Greek king of the gods, was renamed Jupiter by the Romans. Hera, his wife, became Juno.

Romans were great believers in omens. They believed that natural signs, like the sudden appearance of an eagle or an unusual storm, were a warning of important events, such as an earthquake or the death of the **emperor**. They also believed in telling the future by examining the **entrails** of sacrificed birds.

Holidays and festivals

Family occasions

Families could have their own private **festivals** including birthdays, the day the son of the house spoke his first word, or the return of a household member from a journey. Travel was rightly regarded as risky, particularly when it involved a voyage by sea.

Public holidays

Religious festivals were usually public holidays, although business was only forbidden on the most solemn occasions. Festivals usually included games, races and performances of plays. Some of the most important festivals for children and families were:

1st January – bulls were sacrificed to Jupiter for his protection

13th-21st February – past family members' tombs were honoured with flowers, food and wine

15th March – families celebrated the goddess of the year with picnics

21st April – bonfires and street parties honoured Rome's foundation day

24th June – boating parties and picnics honoured Fortuna, goddess of luck

13th August – **slaves** got a day off in honour of Diana, goddess of hunting

A young child holding a goat for sacrifice. The child is wearing a *bulla* around his neck.

Winter festival

As in modern times, the middle of winter was a time of special celebration for parents and their children. The festival of *Saturnalia* extended over a number of days starting on 17th December. It was a time for families to get together and presents were exchanged. Slaves were given special privileges and, for one day, changed places with their masters.

This wall painting from Ostia, Italy, shows children taking part in a religious festival.

Apart from regular festivals there might be additional ones to celebrate a victory in war, or to ask the aid or mercy of the gods in a disaster. Villages celebrated fertility gods and goddesses to mark ploughing, sowing, harvesting and other high points of the agricultural calendar. Farmers led animals round their field boundaries in a procession, then **sacrificed** them while praying to the gods to ward off diseases, storms or drought. Children would have celebrated the harvest as well as adults – it was important for everyone that there was plenty of food to eat.

Lupercalia

Many festivals continued even after Rome became Christian. At *Lupercalia* (15th February) sacrifices were made at the Lupercal, the cave where the wolf sheltered Romulus and Remus. Then young men in goat skin girdles ran through Rome, admired by young girls. To stamp this festival out, in AD 494 Pope Gelasius I banned Christians from taking part. He made the day a festival in honour of the Virgin Mary.

All grown up

Coming of age

A free Roman boy passed to manhood between the age of fourteen and seventeen. The special ceremony of putting on a man's **toga** usually took place in the **forum** at the festival of *Liberalia* on 17 March. Before going there he would offer his *bulla*, and boy's tunic to the gods at the household altar. The whiskers from the new adult's first shave were put in a glass **phial**, and left at the temple of Apollo as an offering. Then he went to a government office to register as a **citizen**, which made him liable for **military service**. Then came a party at home to celebrate. A young man could not hold important public positions until he was thirty, and had done ten years of military service.

Getting married

Girls became women when they became wives. The night before her wedding the bride offered her favourite dolls and toys to the gods at her household **shrine**. Interestingly, Roman dolls were usually made to look like brides, not babies.

A bronze statue of a Roman soldier from the 2nd century AD. It is now in the British Museum. He is wearing an iron helmet, a leather skirt and heavy sandals.

An engraving of a Roman wedding ceremony, from the 2nd century AD. The bridegroom holds the bride's hand.

Parents, especially among wealthy or politically powerful families, usually arranged marriages. Husbands were usually grown men, while brides were normally in their early teens. Engagements were marked with a party and a marriage contract. The contract set out the terms of the **dowry** of cash or land given with the bride. The bride was given a ring, which she wore on the third finger of the left hand. This was because Romans believed that there was a nerve there leading straight back to the heart.

The wedding day had to be chosen to avoid unlucky dates. April and the second half of June were considered especially favourable. On the big day the bride braided her hair and put on a head-dress of flowers, a white tunic and a flame-red veil. Her family home was decorated with flowers and ribbons. When the groom arrived, a priest performed a ritual to make sure the day was still lucky. After an exchange of vows and the signing of the wedding contract, the chief bridesmaid joined the hands of the newlyweds. They then prayed to the gods for their blessing. After a party at the bride's home everybody went in procession to the groom's home, accompanied by torch-bearers and musicians. When they arrived, the groom carried the bride over the threshold and their new life together began.

How do we know?

The problem of the past

Historians try to recapture the past out of what people wrote, made, built or buried. Most of what the Romans wrote or made is lost forever. Common items of wood or wax, clay or cloth, horn, bone or leather are most likely to have rotted. The same is true of papyrus or **parchment**. Much of what has survived has come from late in Roman history, and from Roman Egypt and North Africa, where the dry climate has preserved many objects and manuscripts.

Tombs and treasures

One direct form of evidence about Roman childhood is the burials, bodies and belongings of children themselves. Babies less than forty days old were often just buried under the floor of the house. In the countryside, where most people lived, child burials were equally simple. So little evidence survives about these sort of children. Rich children, however, were buried in fine stone tombs, which often preserved their remains far better. The tombs often contained favourite dolls, toys and, in the case of infants, feeding bottles.

A miniature glass bowl. It was part of the grave goods belonging to a young girl buried in the 3rd century AD. It is amazing that the bowl remains in such good condition.

On display in the Museum of London there are the grave goods found with a young girl who was buried early in the third century AD. Her parents had buried with her a pair of earrings made of loops of twisted gold wire, and a bronze coin that had been worn as a pendant. She also had two white clay figures of the goddess of Venus, an ivory statuette, a miniature glass bowl and a tiny carved bone jar with a lid.

Some tombs have carved portraits. One shows a little girl holding her favourite pet cat. Sometimes pets were buried with the child, perhaps so that they could keep their spirit company. We know much more about rich, powerful, educated Romans – because they had more and could do more – than we do about the poor who outnumbered them by millions. In terms of numbers, the most common type of Roman ever to have lived was a child who died before they could have children of their own.

A father's grief

Inscriptions on tombs show how particularly sad parents were when children had died as teenagers, having survived childhood illnesses. In a letter to a friend, the writer Pliny described how, after the invitations had been sent out, a thirteen year old girl's father was: 'spending on **incense**, perfumes and spices for her funeral what he had planned to spend on gowns, pearls and jewels for her wedding.' She must have come from a wealthy family for her father to plan for such luxury.

The pair of earrings with twisted gold wire that were also found in the grave dating from the 3rd century AD. The grave was found in London.

Timeline

BC

753	Traditional date for the founding of the city of Rome by Romulus
c.600	Latin becomes a written language
509	Last Roman king overthrown in favour of a republic
312	Building work begins on the Via Appia, Rome's first great road
58–50	Julius Caesar conquers Gaul
55–54	Julius Caesar twice invades Britain
44	Julius Caesar is murdered
27	Augustus becomes the first Roman emperor

AD

43	Claudius conquers Britain
73	Major slave uprising led by Spartacus
79	Eruption of Vesuvius buries Pompeii and Herculaneum
80	Colosseum completed
122	Hadrian's Wall built to defend the northern frontier of Britain
165–167	Plague spreads through the empire
395	Roman empire is divided into western and eastern halves
410	Last Roman soldiers leave Britain

Sources and further reading

◄► ◄► ◄► ◄► ◄► ◄► ◄► ◄► ◄► ◄► ◄► ◄► ◄► ◄► ◄► ◄►

Sources

Adults and Children in the Roman Empire,
T. Wiedemann (Yale University Press, 1990)
Daily Life in Ancient Rome,
Jerome Carcopino (Penguin, 1991)
Marriage, Divorce and Children in Ancient Rome,
B. Rawson (Ed.) (Oxford University Press, 1991)
The Oxford Classical Dictionary,
Simon Hornblower and Antony Spawforth
(Oxford University Press,1996)
The Penguin Historical Atlas of Ancient Rome,
Chris Scarre (Penguin, 1995)
Roman Britain,
Peter Salway (Oxford University Press, 1984)
Roman Britain: Life in an Imperial Province,
Keith Branigan (Reader's Digest, 1980)
The Romans, Antony Kamm (Routledge, 1995)
The Roman World, John Boardman, Jasper Griffin and Oswyn Murray
(Oxford University Press,1988)

Further reading

Ancient Rome,
Simon James (DK Publishing, 2000)
Beliefs and Myths of Roman Britain,
Martin Whittock (Heinemann Library, 1997)
Encyclopaedia of the Roman World,
Jane Bingham, Fiona Chandler, Sam Taplin (Usborne, 2002)
Explore History: Romans, Anglo-Saxons & Vikings in Britain,
Haydn Middleton (Heinemann Library, 2001)
The Romans, A.J. Marks and G.I.F. Tingay (Usborne, 1990)
Step into the Roman Empire,
Philip Steele (Anness Publishing, 1997)
What Do we Know About the Romans?
Mike Corbishley (Simon & Schuster, 1991)

Glossary

ancestor family member from long ago

archaeology study of objects and evidence from the past

astronomy study of the stars and planets

barbarian person who did not respect Roman ways

chariot two-wheeled cart used for racing or warfare

citizen Roman man entitled to vote in elections and serve in the legions

concentric circles circles drawn inside each other

death mask portrait made from a wax mould of a dead person's face

divorce break-up of a marriage

dowry gift made to a person getting married

dysentery stomach infection causing a person to go to the toilet repeatedly

emperor supreme ruler of Rome

empire large area with many peoples living under rule of an emperor

entrails insides of the stomach

excavation digging to uncover items from the past

festival celebration, usually in honour of a god

forum large open square in a Roman city, used for public meetings

gambling betting

Germanic something from Germany

gladiator trained professional fighter who fought in the Roman arena

hearth place for a fire

heir person who inherits money and land

hobbyhorse toy made of a long stick with reins and a horse's head

incense something burned to produce a sweet smell

inscription writing cut into wood or stone, usually on a gravestone

legal contract agreement which can be enforced by a law court

linen light, white cloth woven from fibres of the flax plant

loincloth simple form of underwear, a strip of cloth wound around the waist

midwife nurse who helps women have babies

military service being in the army

mosaic decorative picture made up of tiny pieces of coloured tile

mythology and **myths** ancient stories about gods or heroes

parchment a surface for writing on, made from animal skin

phial long, thin glass jar

physician doctor

politics taking part in the decisions made by government

prisoner of war person captured in battle

protective god god who prevents harm

public baths baths open to everyone

republic form of government in early Rome, with elected officials, not a king

rhetoric art of speaking well in public

sacrifice living thing killed in honour of a god

shrine place where gods are worshipped

sinew strand of muscle attached to a bone

slave servant who was not free, and who belonged to a master

slave trader person who bought and sold slaves

spin twist fibres to make thread

stirrup metal ring hung from a saddle for the rider's foot

stylus pointed stick used for writing on wax

swaddled wrapped up tightly in cloth

toga Roman garment, like a loosely folded cloak

tunic sleeveless knee-length garment, often pulled in at the waist

Underworld dark and gloomy place to which Romans believed people went after death

villa large country house

weave interlace thread to make cloth

wet nurse nurse hired to feed a baby with her breast milk

Index